# Clan MacHine

# Clan MacHine

Ian McDonough

Chapman Publishing

2002

Chapman Publishing
4 Broughton Place
Edinburgh EH1 3RX
Scotland

The publisher acknowledges the award
from the Deric Bolton Trust towards
the publication of this volume.

The publisher acknowledges the financial
assistance of the Scottish Arts Council.

A catalogue record for this volume is
available from the British Library.
ISBN 1-903700-01-9

Chapman New Writing Series
Editor Joy Hendry
ISSN 0953-5306

Some of these poems have appeared in the following magazines
and newspapers: *Cencrastus, Chapman, Edinburgh Review, Lines
Review, Northwords, Orbis, Physics News, Poetry Scotland, Scotland
On Sunday, The Scotsman, Spectrum, Times Higher Educational
Supplement, West Coast Magazine* and *Understanding.* 'A Night in
Stoer Lighthouse' and 'Typography in Winter' first appeared in The
Golden Goose Hour (Taranis 1996). 'Sandwood Bay' was first pub-
lished in *A Tribute To Norman MacCaig* (Chapman 1996). 'Back'
and 'Dawn Train' first appeared in *Such Strange Joy* (Inyx 2001).

The author would also like to thank the Scottish Arts Council for
their assistance in the form of a Writers Award in 1999.

Photo by Tara Duncan

Printed by *IBT* Global, 1B Barking Business Centre, 25 Thames
Road, Barking, London IG11 0JP

# Contents

## Further Beyond

## Clan MacHine

*For Ruth*

*and*

*Tuesday Rose*

# Introduction

Many writers draw copiously on the environment they grew up in. Rural and remote settings especially can lend colour for its own sake, or induce either nostalgia or such subjectivity as excludes the wider world. Among the joys of Ian McDonough's new collection is its breadth of perspective. While vividly evoking the loch-littered, sparsely populated Sutherland of his upbringing he encompasses a rich canvas of physical and spiritual elements and relationships.

From the opening lines he presents the actuality and feel of his heartland with poise and precision. Such are his imaginative energy and originality that he makes the place strikingly his own. He displays an uncanny empathy with those figures, real or ghostly (the drowned sailors in 'A Night in Stoer Lighthouse'), who inhabit his poems. And 'Salt Street', in which he himself appears, is just one of many glistening pieces whose taut lyricism is attuned to the inner vision of a true poet.

Exhilarating too are his linking of past and present, and sense of our lives being at the mercy of external forces. But whether on the high crags of Assynt or scanning space, he retains a tight focus. His gulls wheel over specific rocks as well as under remote galaxies. He pinpoints the fragility of a "tea-cup, cradled like a linnet's egg". And throughout hover vestiges of folk memory - and often-unexpected spillages of humour.

Some of the most recent poems probe the boundaries between art and science, and themes these may not at first appear to share. The intuitive leaps of the one are set against the inspiration, and searching for truth, of the other. Then he pulls from his hat the Clan MacHine sequence which gives the volume its title. Fantastical yet down to earth, as if corralled in some extravagant theme-park of the mind, their eccentric logic and pastimes are described with wit and ingenuity; 'The First MacHine in Space', on which he ends, positively leaping from the page.

Ian McDonough's enquiring mind, lightness of touch yet seriousness of purpose and above all his warmth make this volume for me not just highly accomplished and entertaining, but adventurous and deeply rewarding.

*Stewart Conn*

# Sutherland

## Back

Rainwater and memory
pool in the hollows,
sew a silky skin
over pocked and littered lanes,
irradiate
the dark and shuttered suburbs
of sidereal time.

Inside, a swelling tide of talk
rushes the photo-studded walls,
washes into attics,
refreshing desiccated hurts and treasures.
Neurons, long asleep, fire up
like old toy racing cars,
batteries
surging with fresh volts.

Wading out into the coddling night,
I try to shake the voice
of my integral guide
blethering weathered histories
inside my saturated head.

*This village is the sea that spawned you.*
*This house is the boat that launched you.*
*This body is the lighthouse*
*that you sail around, and to, and from.*

# Fishing off Brora

Out of shore's sight, a sudden grey
The wrinkling water taps on hollow wood
In the echo-chamber of a floating firth.

A sudden quiet, an ectoplasmic haar
The wrinkled wood slaps water hard
We jump, a gull takes umbrage, flies,
Disgusted by the hollow heart of land.

## A Night in Stoer Lighthouse

Here a hungry man
could chew up the Atlantic
and still feel need of salt.

Can you smell the sun go down?
Extend a surreptitious hand to touch
the moon's deep cavities? A fox
surrounds the lighthouse with its bark.

Your body sprouts tattoos
of whaling ships: the eiderdown is sea-haar,
bedposts timbers decked in weeds.

I reach under green sheets to dredge
a bucketful of sailors, drowned
as drowned can be. A prowling moth
flaps round the lightbulb
in a breeze, traversing
all the open oceans of our dreams.

Blood atmospheres return, the walls
recalled by seagull tides of dawn. The fox
is earthed: the sun erects its peepshow
in a fragrant void.

# Jacob's Ladder

The minister aims the missiles of his wrath
and serpents lodge in congregated throats,
draining moisture out of souls already parched.

Bright morning drums its fingers on stained glass.
The minister wills his sweat to turn to blood,
hearing, outside, the sea and pagan air kiss deep.

Hauled by the precentor's writhing rope
the congregation rise to scale a psalm,
filling local hearts with lofty Israel's woes.

But Jacob Beag, opening his
mouth to tow the line,
feels a salt trickle in his throat
and hears an ocean drown the praise with sound.

Blackness. Then blinding light. The visions come
– not of a New Jerusalem and the Lamb,
but summer nights, his wife, his croft, a favourite spade.

# A Walk across the Cleared Areas

*Altanduin*

The ruined land
is whispering its history
to switchback streams
boundless sky.

*Tuarie*

By Strath na Frith
the past is darkening.
Pockets of sun
    illuminate
a bare-stoned future.

*Achrintle*

Where children sang
wraith mists
an empty moon.

*Badanraffan*

Sunk in ferns
shadow homesteads
    indistinct
something not-quite-remembered.

*Ascoile*

The path dips
into activity,
worked land.
Looking back,
a sign – "Danger – Stalking in Progress".

# NATO Fleet – Moray Firth

All that whole day, it was only the empty hill
could hear me whistle for the sake of company.

Unless I count one hare, prim and fast as sound,
which tore across the heather in its high disgust.

From above Brora the firth was a pristine tablecloth
speckled with frigates, cruisers, battleships,
as though some anxious host had laid
an over-ostentatious cruet set. The midges

droned on and on. Below, the gunboats glinted
quietly, almost pretty in their hostile finery.

And I thought about the stinging kingdoms of the world
till, trying to whistle down the hill, I fell quite dumb.

## Salt Street

Ice crinkles underfoot, shuts the river's mouth,
winks at us everywhere we look. Beached craft,
gift-wrapped in tinsel, creak like haunted shacks
as up and down my spine gaunt walkers leave their tracks.

The Moray Firth flings up a violet plume of cloud:
our prospect glazes, crystal breathlessly descends.
Then, weighted like a boxer's unanticipated blow,
a heaving gale brings cryogenic seas of snow.

Your hand grips tighter as the saturating chill
slides underneath your coat, stabs into your small bones.
I pick you up and run, directionless, along my childhood street,
losing the place where history and vision used to meet.

Safe inside the living room your widening eyes light up
as black hearth gods consume their ancient lives.
I pull a switch, the television channels climb
like spiders over webs of latitude and longitude and time.

## Sandwood Bay

The fat silences of the world
have landed on the beach
for their Annual Conference.
This year the theme is silence.

After a hectic schedule
of no speeches, no workshops
and no discussion-panels,
the delegates quietly depart.

"Save me from pantheistic tourists!"
sighs the sea, resuming
its unstructured, profane clamour.

## *The Slide*

Overnight, the brae behind our playground
snapped to ice: we polished – polished
till a bright-black film of danger
swallowed the innocent light.

This game was compulsory, no parental
lines. First down chipped a tooth,
the second blacked her eye, I knocked
my senses haywire for an hour.

Techniques improved through observation,
trial and error – don't look down,
think of something else, don't rush it –
till even the gallumphers kept their feet.

Then the refinements – one leg,
backwards, eyes tight shut,
the group descents. Tricks got riskier
as we felt a thaw approach.

Tricks get riskier now, as I sense
thawing in my bones, and dare
infrequent glances down to where
my shoes attempt to grip the hurtling ice.

## Mrs Wilson Sunrise opens the Fête

A sanity of tweed is pressing the rebellious ground
beneath a kindly brogue which moderates all pace.
She stops to cock an ear and register the timbre of the day –
a gentle clack of hoopla, thwack of darts, dark sausage hiss.
All is as it should be – drizzle is expected soon.

Mrs Wilson Sunrise scissors through the taut red tape
to sounds of dropping balls and creaking stays.
The band strikes up 'There is a Green Hill Far Away'.
She dreams of tidal waves, of Strauss and 'Four Last Songs',
but all is as it should be – drizzle is expected soon.

# Vertigo, Craggan Rock

Dark turbulences sweetly pull my eyes
down to where nothing but bare promise
keeps the air from swallowing the sun.

Everything I know of trails back from
this place: at first the single strand of now,
fraying itself into a split and twisted then,

and back still further till again it weaves
itself into one crucial cord, connecting
absence to the glimmer of a waking state.

Nothing looms more horribly than nothing.
Below the sparrows and the sparrow-hawks
breast the soundless gap, sleepwalking through

their unrecorded histories. Here the future
is as sheer as glass, waiting for a signature
to etch its conscious handhold on the void.

# *Dreaming of Being with You in Glengolly*

Maybe it was just being there, the light,
the time of year, the room
you coughed yourself to death in.

I had been in a land of black stars,
torn down by an affair pursued in violent skies,
and now I felt your presence everywhere.

Dreaming of walking with you in Glengolly,
before Dunkirk, tuberculosis,
and the slamming doors of pain.
With waterfalls running sweetly through your veins,
your frame as weatherproof as silver birch –
the world as easy as a meadow.

I want to reach back through the glass of years,
bring you comfortable breezes,
give myself some rest.

Dreaming of being with you in Glengolly
I woke, to find that you had calmed
a windswept hillside of my emptiness.

## Moving the Caravan

Out of the snail-backed hills
a lorry descended, civilisation
on its deck. When we arrived
it had been as though a tooth
were missing from a favourite smile.
One of the scattered beat-up boxy caravans
had gone, its floor succumbing
after years of gales and footsteps.
Now a new family member had appeared.

We joined the anxious owner, driver,
several moths attracted by the flame.
It was a task, like all tasks here,
needing careful contemplation, planning,
before the irreversibility of action.
Mechanical winch fused with muscle, tilting
the new van one way, then another, till
angles being just so, it slid firmly home.

The owner grinned, our driver smiled and drove:
ropes were attached, stakes driven,
boulders piled. Then we left the caravan alone
to start its patient contest
with that Sutherland air,
a winner never in question,
only the length of the game.

## Past Dancing

And this is almost no word
of a lie. Men with boots
like sky there were,
the women
prancing feathers in a gale.

Long tunes too.
Not once round the hall
and see you at the bar –
but most of them a good year long,
and that was just the verse.
If the refrain came,
you were in for a century at least.

People lived and died
during the one tune.
A particularly memorable hornpipe,
it is told,
saw the waxing
and the waning
of an entire civilisation.

Neighbours lost their sleep,
protesting
that their dogs,
their bairns and sheep,
were red-eyed in the morning.

But did we take offence
at such unmusical discourtesy?
In truth
there was no time
with every minute at the dancing.

It stopped when we wore out the floor
– and, underneath the boards,
found bones of other creatures
who had danced away the dawn
until their dancing days were done.

# No Mad Men

*The New Statistical Account of the parish of Clyne reports that in the year of 1840 there are five mad women and no mad men.*

Clynemilton burn in spate – brown gobs of foam
race downwards to the Autumn sea. Leaves turn
on trees: it is so late, and still daft Katie lies in bed.
Her cow bleats like a bairn, hens frenzy at the sun –
Reverend Mackay is told. Something must be done.

Magga counts her blessings, ends before she starts.
Ghosts of sickly children croup and huddle round
an icy hearth. Married into strangers in this strangers'
strath, husband gone to serve the Queen, she walks
her agonies along the shore: a whispering starts.

Jeannie Mhor, fat Jeannie, fecund, grimed with soot,
gathers a happy, swarming brood and dances round
the stones of her domain. Whisky in her veins and all
her world is gay, obliterating memory of childhood
beatings, rape. A passing neighbour watches, waits.

The study of the manse is running damp. He hunkers
on his knees – Lord purify the soul that countenances
thoughts like these. The tacksman of Kilbraur arrives
scarlet with tales of shame. Tonight the minister will
dream of women dancing, naked, sodden in the rain.

Euphemia Gordon, widow of Ascoile, heavy of purse
and light of sense, removes the corpses of the starlings
from the lawn. Eyes everywhere, she slaughters anything
that dares to spy on her affairs. The minister brings
sympathy, takes sugared tea and lingers on and on.

Dolina mends a net of souls and sings at stars – black
visions burn the pupils of her eyes. The wind's boat
ploughs a furrow through the muddy skies – men of
the cloth lie hidden in the grass, the women's skirts
are high. Blood roars inside her ears in swelling tides.

Clynemilton burn in spate – brown gobs of foam
race downward to the winter sea. The unbewildered
men allow restraint, arrange four women's transport
through the poorhouse door. The minister and widow
lift their tea, express a measured portion of their sympathy.

## Pollan

Green finches fill the bushes
On the road up to Pollan
High above a speckle of lochans
Where the yellow trout are jumping.

Two fir trees in the garden
Of the cottage at Pollan
A prospect from the window
Of the high crags of Assynt.

The sun dances on peaks
Water moves like molten iron
I could live a thousand years
In the soft light of Pollan.

# Sutherland and Beyond

## A New Life

The man whose clothes I stole
is running naked
through the back streets of my brain.

He is shouting at the top
of my voice . . . "Stop him,
the thieving bastard!"
. . . but knows
that only he and I are listening.

I have some surprises in store
for the naked man.
Soon, heavy snow showers
will begin to fall, and the wind
will get up a little. Naturally,
it will emanate from the North.

Why am I so mean to him? Why
are my streets so cold,
so charmlessly bereft
of the milk of human kindness?

Because these garments, garish,
preposterous, outlandish, gauche,
have wrapped themselves
so tightly round my bones,
I tear and tear
but cannot rip them off.

## Melting Weather

Out of season, snow covered all our year
and nothing leaving footprints walked
the earth. It was a time for fires,
hoarding up our blessings,
checking children, damping down desires,
for reading rusty entrails of slow clocks.

But today it has arrived, the melting weather:
snowmen weep themselves to death
in every garden. Tomorrow all that lingers
will be buttons, pipes and scarves,
half-hidden in the springing grass.

We have had enough of snowmen, whispering
cold nothings in drowsy ears,
winking at the children, spreading
icy fingers on the treasures of the heart.

Still we wait inside, reluctant to emerge
and greet the melting weather, guessing that
returning, we might find doors barred,
snowmen snuggled by the fire. And us
out there with buttons, pipes and scarves

rooted to the winter ground,
discovering our eyes
have smithereened to frosted glass.

## Inverness

Like the clumping of galaxies,
much of the raw matter of the Highlands
has been drawn inexorably together.

Gull patrols wheel and squawk,
mirroring interminable, edgy talk
ricocheting between the thronging pubs.

Someday we all will leave. Meanwhile
folk memories glint in speech, bright tormentil
among the prosaic, spreading heather.

## Holburn Head, Caithness

What has this to do with nations?
With the culture branded
like a laceration on our skin?
These cliffs do not aspire from
nor fall into the sea, and neither
do they poison children with their songs
of gallantry in death. This wind does not
howl like a banshee on Culloden moor,
but forms its sound by beating up the air,
where gulls fly white as sheets
against a blue Atlantic, signalling
a saltire for the first and last of states.

## Landed

North Roe wore that familiar, old grey ganzy
as I signalled down
to where the sea ran like a train
and turquoise shimmered
at the feet of cliffs.

Then you said
    "Yes, but I want turquoise everywhere."

Later,
the bar was like a lobster-pot,
with all of Shetland
waiting for a grizzled fisherman
to winch them up into the light.

## Columba in the North

Straths curl like tapeworm through
the big-boned hills. No guiding light
among the paths that weave dark spells
beyond the reach of ordinary sight.
Hovels perch like carrion
beneath a filthy moon which soaks
the earth with bestial longings of the night.
Strengthen my arm to flay this land
into a revelation of the Word.
Fill their huts with terror
at the many-coloured raiments of the Lord.

After the sea-crossing, marching north,
my soul stretched out like skin. Visions
of grace dissolved into strange ardours,
shameless in their wild profanity.
Last night I dreamed The Lamb had rent
this land asunder with His sword, then
cursed its spilling blood as He consumed
its flesh. Each day I test my mettle
on a heathen dawn, cutting a swathe
through stinging thistles to my God.

## Listening to Dionne Warwick

As if in answer to the blues, it gets misty.
The Crags shake their skirts then disappear
across a flattened, disapproving Central Belt
to meet their down-home country lovers,
hanging loose and snowy-haired around Glencoe.

Trumpets weave their counterpoint to the elemental song.
I trace your outline in the fading gloom,
wishing this tenement would pick up its old skirts and run
past Queensferry, Perth, Drumochter, Inverness,
nudging me down beside you on that Caithness beach.
The record turns itself, and plays 'A House is not a Home'.

# Hill-Shepherd in a Tearoom

Bolt upright, a dun-suited beacon
endures the sea of paisley pattern,
daisy print and ivory lace.
Only the eyes move, straining
to demolish walls, burn out some space.

The tea-cup – cradled like a linnet's egg
inside the rawness of his grasp –
must break, and flood the tearoom
with a spate of sepia dye.

And tables, chairs and chintzy walls
will turn to undelineated moor,
revealing only to the weathered eye
a million tiny riots of bloom
bursting out of heather, rock and moss.

## William Gillies

In Temple village
the hill runs steeply
past your door.
A carnival of kids,
of hoops and dolls,
of woolly village dogs,
looks straight at you,
not seeing –
as you perceive only too well –
a half-hewn scarlet bogeyman
tramping down the cobblestones
to gobble up your fuzzy summer light.

## The Sea's Invitation to Dance

Come, you with such warm blood
throbbing gently in your temples,
can you not see me shiver?
It is an ancient coldness in my veins.

Do you not hear me beat my heart
to pieces on the shore?
I have such a story to reveal –
let me dance, dance with you.
The wind will whip us into feeling.

Later we will lie below the light,
saturated, bloated with our love.
Give me your hand, your hand my dear.
Soon we will begin to waltz.

## Typography in Winter

Mark your words on me, the spread
of pristine snow commanded urgently.
We hopped the dyke
to scrawl a wish.

Near the gate, we found
a different story written bold.
Four small paws scurrying desperate yards,
edge of a wing –
a talon-scratch.

Then nothing but the dreadful snow.

# *Thurso: Sunday Evening Post-Election*

At the mainland's top edge,
where North Sea and Atlantic
stream together,
we feel the tide
has finally turned our way.

And still the streets
are smothered in a rain so dense
the darkness is a black confetti
tossed over the mirrored ground.

The town clock bangs away another hour.
A rising wind deals out random tattoos of sleet
against each window pane.
Change grips your throat like ozone.

## Sunday Gesture

After an early morning bottle of sherry
He strolled down to the village
Walked up the aisle of a crowded church
And, aiming his shotgun at the organist
Made him play
     'I Do Like To Be Beside The Seaside'.

God, in his wisdom, did not intervene,
Knowing farce to be immune to bolts of lightning.
The police took a dimmer view.

## At the Astronomy Lecture

Comet Shoemaker-Levy 9 is waving its long hair
at students sparse and scattered out as galaxies,
lost in a stomach-churning loneliness
the better-balanced of us filter out from observation.

Out on his own, desolate as one of Pluto's moons,
circled by Co-op carrier bags, anorak an atmospheric
earthy blue, another comet shakes his streaks of hair
and probes our lecturer – *What if an undetected rock
should dip to craze our orbit irrevocably?*

The lecturer admits a distant chance, but won't lose sleep.
The comet crashes,
fires extinguished by cheap jokes.
And softly, guiltily, we leave, knowing
what really has been asked by this stray body
who has scanned the heavens looking for a home,
and, finding none, called down the gods of chaos.

## Holiday Cottage, Auchencairn

The pans, the Superspeed electric cooker,
coffee table, rusty two-bar fire, were
once the fierce familiars of an ideal home.
Ghosts of monopoly nights, of singsongs,
Chinese burns, of Daddy's little jokes,
moan softly behind mildewed floral skin.
We are the scouts of some untutored outland
tribe, squinting at livid paintings,
berserk lampshades, paperbacks stuffed full
of love and doom. Outside a robin simpers,
hyacinths run measured circles round
the pampered lawn: an island, sporting ruins
and a lighthouse sits a pretty distance
from the shore. Everything is pinned down tightly
in its place against that ruinous breeze
which blew the wide, wide world so far off course.

## Dawn Train

Through parted clouds
the world's wound gapes,
viscera
streaked across the sky.

Even the old among us
wince and gasp,
as morning's insurrection
demands we heave and strain,
our bodies briefly
too large for their frames.

Like a ripped tent,
night admits
a stream of photons.
Blood stirs and agitates,
then boils,
in the arterial scarlet of another day.

## Playing Cards on the Computer

To-day as always, I am playing Alex, Ken and Julie.
Each of us is trying to lose all of our Hearts,
or else to win them all and clinch it with
the Queen of Spades. Like all good games,
it is both simple and hard, a blend of skill and luck.
Alex, Ken and Julie are a pretty even match –
I have been losing frequently but I am fighting back.

Only I exist. Sometimes I sense that Alex is pushy,
Ken calmer, Julie more the strategist, but know
that I am reading random number generations.
Who am I playing against? A programmer? Myself?
No-one? The thought makes me switch off, seeing
an endless evening of the world, where Romeos
sing like grasshoppers to their Juliet reflections.

# Border Ballad

The moon, which borders
on a state knowing no reason,
swings over mountains with impunity.

Swings between coyness
and a lusty streak across the sky,
falls drunk into the hissing sea,
gets itself arrested by the dawn.

Gets itself banned
from the Cartographic Society
for changing the names of its oceans
into a language of static interference.

The moon, which glows like treasure
but is larded up with dust,
beams a cheesy smile on midnight ramblers,
licks the bare backsides of lovers.

Cares not a jot that some big toothy grin
has stuck a flag into its skin.
Or that it is judged a harsh mistress
by the soft and mistressless.

The moon has a voice so low
it opens your bowels, breaks your teeth,
shoves your astral readings
where the sun will never shine.

The moon borders on a state of mind
without the hindrance of a mind.

## Brickworks Road

Pooled in black light
The river's elbow lifts and falls
Round a steep brambled rise
Where fruit sports sulphur dust
Air is the devil's breath
Turning washing into saffron robes.

A whistle blows.
Looming from the yellowed earth,
Badger-men, wild, red-eyed,
Lumbering back towards our homes.

## The Memory of Water

In the quiet times,
snowdrifts high outside,
nothing comes to mind
but the memory of water.

Remember how it moves so
swiftly through the world,
and how its mirrored
surface holds your gaze.

How currents warm its
molecules, dissolve the
icy fissures threading
through your frozen days.

In the crystal times,
white and paralysed,
feel the itch of spring –
the alchemy of water.

# Further Beyond

## Strathclyde University Physics Department

Today I am propelled out of Queen Street Station
to find Glasgow basking in the radiation
of a class G2V Yellow Dwarf.

In the Colville Building, monks and nuns
of the sub-atomic orders scribble in their cells.
The corridors flash with exotic, glancing interactions.

Like an atheist concealed among the cloisters,
I struggle through weak forces, leptons, quarks,
ears ringing with the plainsong of an alien world.

But this is our world. The quantum testaments,
more cryptic than a Gnostic text, reveal the workings
of transistors, electricity, our household techno-Gods.

Labs hum with prayers of femtosecond lasers.
How many angels fit a pinhead? It depends
on where you make your observation from.

Walking, dazzled, back along Cathedral Street,
the G2V Yellow Dwarf eclipsed by passing clouds,
my mind is lit by tracer-fires of faith.

# Two Poems for Boris Chertok

*Chertok, an enigmatic and witty physicist, was second in command of the Soviet Space Programme during much of the Cold War.*

## Vocation

Russia, 1926, an aimless boy
strays into a seedy picture hall.
A Martian princess, Aelita,
decorates the flecked and fuzzy screen.
Besieged by bug-eyed traitors,
she needs rescued, double quick.

Ever since, the aimless boy
has aimed his rockets
at a flecked and fuzzy sky.

## Search for Life

Seeking out Martians, but prepared
to settle for bacteria,
the Soviets launched an early probe
to the Red Planet.

Before the launch, cautious as ever,
Chertok checked the life-detector out
in downtown Kazakhstan.
Not even a flicker.

## Einstein's Head

Shelved in a back room
of Madam Tussaude's,
there it lay in its field of white curls.
Eyes radiating,
it gazed through the walls
to where the waxy body
was melted and transformed
into another transitory star.

It seemed his public weight
had dipped below the critical mass,
and like all arriving at this state,
his time in the light had passed.

Who could replace this musician,
magician, comic, philosopher,
this reluctant politician
unearthing wonders so strange
even he could not believe them fully?

What does it mean
when we sever the heads
of those who connect us
to our generation, our flux,
our nemesis?

## Microwave Detectors

The atmosphere is singing as you walk,
through infra-red and UHF
to buy your oranges and bread.

An orchestra of frequencies
is playing inside your blinded head
each time you cook, play ball
or dance the cha-cha-cha.

In the quiet of your early room,
at the bottom of the undersea,
we reach out tendrils to detect
a small exchange of energies.

We are waving to you,
hearken to the agitated air.

Stillness is a vacuum,
a weary monkish trick.
Motion, the true signature of life,
infiltrates, resonates everywhere.

## Poised to Exist

In a dressing room behind the stage
A graviton preens itself
Checks that its symmetry is not slipping
Waits for the curtain call.

It is in an excited state, having heard
That its existence has been postulated
By the theory of N=8 Supersymmetry
In the stalls, calculating physicists fidget and wait.

The graviton is ghostly, small and faint
And like uncertain actors everywhere
Defines its being only through an audience
The physicists prepare a spontaneous standing ovation.

## Red Shift

Bounded by the womb
distance signifies nothing to us
until,
convulsed
towards the heavy light
of planets,
we enter measurement.

# Chain of Capacitors

Pathways of approximation
crisscross labs and borders,
weave in and out of laptops,
enter memory banks and texts.

Calibration, gearing, tuning,
a subtle instruction of machines,
topping and tailing, engineering
our smooth administration
of this wilful universe.

Nothing can replicate exactly.

Sophistry? No, or only rarely.
Approximations turn our wheels,
govern the exodus of knowledge,
free us from being local emperors
ruling in lonesome castles of the self.

A chain of capacitors
sparks and crackles across the labs,
distributing a charge of faith
in what we read, in what we send,
in what we darkly apprehend and measure.

# Invisible Piper

*Human beings, vegetables or cosmic dust; we all dance to a*
*mysterious tune, intoned in the distance by an invisible piper*
— Albert Einstein

Before there were hillsides
Or setting suns to sillhouette his form,
Before there was form,
Before protons and neutrons combined,
His figures transmitted
Through the amniotic fluid
And out of their articulation
Everything was born.

Pibroch, repeating and never-repeating,
Folds on itself – grace-notes doubling,
Generating triplets,
Spawning child universes,
Populating galaxies with sweet cacophony.

After the hillsides lose their form,
And suns collapse, hissing,
After the stuff of matter has dissolved,
Echoes of a fleeting fugue
Will resonate, diminishing,
Throughout the glens of utter space,
Until again he lifts his pipes,
And blows a different storm.

# *A Theory of Everything*

Unlike the duck-billed Platypus,
an egg-laying mammal careless
of its status as a paradox, we worry.

Worry most when certainties collide –
quantum mechanics and general relativity
crashing head-on like snooker balls
to glance away, wholly irreconciled.

Worry ourselves a model of quantum gravity,
write 'string' theories, posit varying speeds
of radiation, foams of black holes,
birthing a universal rule to bind up
and describe us all.

Describe but not explain. What could explain
why danger draws us, why wood is pleasing
to the touch, the tendency of my balls
to swing sometimes one way
sometimes the other,
why sunsets make us weep.

## The Wiggler

In the belly-wrenching gloom
of a bone-strewn cave
Homo Habilis stirred.
His brain was itching.

In sleep he had rolled against
a shard of sharpened bone,
lacerating his side. A sole stray thought
received a kick, radiated light
in a blaze of directions.

With time, he learned
to tune the light.

I lean on bone. I bleed.
The animal who leans on bone
will bleed. Take animal to bone –
it bleeds.

Cause and effect fly,
unstoppable, out of the cave.
Wiggle bone, wiggle stone, wiggle me.
Wiggle my tongue – electrons wiggle
in a penetrating stream
banishing darkness from the cave.

The wiggler, wiggling the world.

# Dark Matter

*Galaxies seem to contain much greater mass than can be accounted for by their stars. This 'invisible' matter remains, as yet, undetected.*

"Adrian?" family and neighbours weighed him up,
"Steady as a clock!" You could plot his orbit
round the well-presented village to the minute.
Work at the Water Board, two pints
at the Bantam Cock, Sunday lunch at Mam's.

Artless, boy and man – fond of his wee nieces,
played a bit of bowls, could take a joke –
ticked on. The village spread around him
like a cloak. He wore it stoically, knew its
twists and turns, the rough warp of its cloth,
its power of insulation. He took to reading books.

One summer Sunday he missed lunch. They found him,
stock still, in Grigson's field, staring at the sky,
eyes engraved with horror. Never said another word
until he died, undiagnosed, the following July.

## The Quark Sisters

Yes, you may date us, but let us say at once
that we are many, some strange, others
displaying bags of charm. Perhaps you know
we always go around the place in threes?

Sometimes we may be up, sometimes,
like anyone, we may be down.
We are all shapely, though some display
more bottom, some more top.

Our favourite colours? No, the only colours
we can wear are red, green, blue. We do not speak
of our half-sisters, the anti quarks, who hussy around
in yellow, magenta and cyan.

Still interested? Then follow up our tracks.
But please don't try to get our knickers down.
Remember, we go about in threes.
You could never afford it.

## Flight To Kirkwall

Just say time flows in streams of particles –
not continuous, but moving
in groups like buses
with nothing in between.

And at rare junctions we could hop like frogs
from one stream to the next,
diving back and forwards between spaces
in the seconds, minutes, years.
How many of each of us
would there be?

Waiting in the airport lounge
I feel the self I had been forty years ago
tugging at my sleeve.
"Remember me? I was the seed
from which you sprouted so profusely
like some common weed."

By the coffee stand I glimpse
another closer self.
He beckons me.
His eyes are halls of mirrors.

Panic lands,
a Spitfire crazed by Messerschmitts.

I conjure hosts of selves
who split their cells,
breeding like seething maggots
in my hollow shell.

## Beam Splitter

We are all servants of the light,
and in the darkness crave it –
the priest who draws down
heaven's fire, the scientist
deciphering signatures
of stars, an artist
ploughing in the colourfield,
a child confounded by the sun.

Ark of the Covenant, save us.
Special Theory of Relativity, save us.
Direction of time, save us.

Lens-grinder, astronaut,
fisherman, diamond-thief,
gardener, midwife,
coal miner, cook.
Fleeing upwards to the fire,
our lives split and diffracted,
we hurtle, massless, through the ancient night.

We are all servants of the light,
and in the darkness crave it.

## The Last Physicist

Having exhausted the possible
Names of God,
Been infinite in a nutshell,
Proved that E
Only usually equals mc$^2$

And having subjugated
The entire particle zoo,
Run time's arrow ragged,
Broken entropy's hold for good,
He switched the lights off,
Cried himself to sleep.

# Clan MacHine

## Clan MacHine

The glen of appliances hums softly in the gloaming.
Bells ring, the clan body salivates, skirmishing
back to the visitor centre. It is empty now,
our pens have been strewn with fresh straw-substitute.

Round Ben Badh the wind's accordion is wheezing
fit to suffocate. In the small hours they say
its voice can drive men mad. There was a piper once,
arose and ripped the chips and wires from his bag.

He blew up such a din the clan began to dance,
stamping on the Collietrons until they smoked and sparked.
The keepers came to pacify the glen with air-conditioning,
replaced the Collietrons and banned the playing
                                           of instruments.

Small hoovers follow footsteps everywhere, sucking up
the detritus which sometimes falls from underneath
men's kilts. We are a small clan, but a clean one.
Whiles I dream that I have climbed Ben Badh
and wake up whistling between my teeth.

# A Lullaby of the Clan MacHine

Hush now, the glen is sleeping

Keepers are in lodges, listening
To their treasure drinking

Ben Badh's wind is hunting
But the door is barred

This is the only world
You are the only child

The rest is dreaming

# *Three Games of the Clan MacHine*

Eleven of the clan pursue a sphere
also pursued by eleven Keepers.
The sphere is charged
with a powerful symbolic intensity.
It is also charged with a magnetic force –
The Keepers wear large magnets in their boots.

At unpredictable intervals,
in order to decide a pre-arranged issue,
a gathering of The Clan and Keepers will occur.
Keepers stand to one side,
observe The Clan do battle with itself
and return home, having secured a standing majority.

When two or more of the clan are gathered,
they are prone to speculate
on whether an unconfirmed, invisible presence
is coloured green or blue.
This game is dogged by frequent injury.

# A MacHine Writes Home from the Asylum

The clouds here frequently collide
And clang like bells.
This scares us
As we have short memories.

On Wednesdays the Duchess comes
To eat our language
As it leaves our mouths.
She is a fat lady.

Out in the yard
Our keepers have us whistle
At the shooting stars
Which tear our sky
In faithless, brief trajectories.

The dung of prowling Collietrons
Is used to help our grass grow blue.
They growl when someone learns
To count past forty-five.

To-day the smell of sheep
And craft-shop candles
Was distilled for us to eat.
The flatulence
May last for years.

Cuckoo-clocks flap through the glen
Drowning out the sound
Of famous corpses shouting
That they are not dead
But only sleeping.

Send a postcard of Ben Badh.
It lumbers through
Our blackened dreams
Trailing its roots
Like an extracted tooth.

The clouds here frequently collide
And clang like bells.
We have short memories . . .
We have short memories . . .

## Why the Clan MacHine Abandoned Accountancy

If twenty comes
And twenty goes
Make forty wents
And wents
Are one pound each
We will be rich
But have no time
To hunt the stag
Or linger
On the beach.

# MacHine Global Systems Corporation
## (www.exodus.com)

Does your fledgling nation
lack a certain sparkle?
Are your heroes
just a little
short on backbone?
Click here
to view our selection
of "Bonnie Scottish Soldiers".
Your streets can be instantly awash
with streams of torrid blood.
At a little extra cost
it may not even be your own.

Double click
on the icon of the Presbyterian manse
to register for our deluxe
guilt-enhancement service.
We guarantee your nation's psyche
will emerge tortured and fascinating,
attracting the profitable interest
of a generation of New World scholars.

If your fiscal health
provokes the jests of merchant bankers,
please click on the icon
of a moth emerging from a dog-eared wallet.
Our tried and tested suite of economic measures
establishes a pleasing asymmetrical distribution
of your hard-earned spoils.
(Warning: certain programmes are susceptible
to the *Revolting Peasant* virus. If detected,
click immediately on the 'Bonny Scottish Soldiers' icon.)

The MacHine Corporation
wishes you to realise
we are your honest sonsie friend.
Click on the icon
of the lifted kilt
to view our specialist sites.

Does your nation's literature
lack an urban kailyard zing?
Your football team
have an undeveloped sense of tragedy?
Are your populace
sentimentally attached
to the wrecked and destitute?
We aim to help you.
We are your honest sonsie friend.

To quit this site please click twice
on the icon of the empty whisky bottle.
The MacHine Corporation
wishes to thank you for your time,
for which we have not yet charged you.

# A MacHine Enters the Virtual Forest

Masts of fibreglass and pine:
the resins weep into fine worm-free ground.
See yon far cut-glass mountain glinting underneath a UV sun?
It crawls with static virtual mountaineers, precipitating
phantom avalanches with their tongue.

Inside the air-conditioned glade a corporate hermit
tinkers with his life-support machine, adjusts
his intravenous drip of sugared barley-bree.
He scatters hazelnuts of wisdom to the squirrels
for a reasonable fee.

And round the virtual forest-paths the virtual tourists run,
averting perfect virtual eyes
from needles littered round the forest-floor.

The Keep of Heritage (admission virtually free)
plays tapes of pipers forging virtual notes,
and sells authentic forest muck to fresh-faced scholars
keen to blacken up.

Deep in the braveheart of the inner wood,
a carbon-fibre cross flashes its runes
and shows an endless video of ancestors who slew their Gods
to live inside a waking state.

## The First MacHine in Space

Boys, it was something
And it was nothing.
Silent as a pinewood
Blacker than the Corrie-Dhu
On a moonless December
Cold as a manse.
Damn the bit of smell.

Boys, the earth was a midge
On the face of Ben Badh
And a cloud of suns
Hung like stags' breath
In the iron morning.
A kilt of stars
Bound it all together
In a pattern
A man could read forever
And never find the match.

Boys, what was it like?
The longest sermon ever penned
Delivered in an unknown tongue
To a congregation of the deaf
In an echoing prison of a church
Without a floor or walls or roof.

## *Biographical Details*

Born in Brora, Sutherland, Ian McDonough has held various jobs, some stranger than others, but now works as a community mediator. He is Convenor of Edinburgh's Shore Poets and co-edited their anthology *The Ice Horses* (Scottish Cultural Press). In 1999 he was awarded a Scottish Arts Council Writer's Bursary and the poem sequence 'A Rising Fever' was published by Kettilonia (2000). He was commissioned by the Engineering and Science Research Council and Strathclyde University to write a series of poems on particle physics, exhibited at the Scottish Poetry Festival, St Andrews, the Mitchell Library, Glasgow and the Traverse Theatre, Edinburgh. His first play *51 Pegasus* is in production with Grey Coast Theatre Company, being developed for a national tour. He lives in Edinburgh. *Clan MacHine* is Ian McDonough's first collection.